What Glorious Possibilities

What Glorious Possibilities

Jim Zola

Kelsay Books

© 2014 Jim Zola. All rights reserved. This material may not be reproduced in any form, published, reprinted, recorded, performed, broadcast, rewritten or redistributed without explicit permission of Jim Zola. All such actions are strictly prohibited by law.

ISBN 13: 978-0615958354

Cover Photo: Jim Zola

Kelsay Books
Aldrich Press
24600 Mountain Avenue 35
Hemet, California 92544

*You work the first shift. Expectations
are petty theft, laziness. You think
of Bird's be-bop and swing, the first mover*

*unmoved, where every story begins
with once upon a time. Think of the voice
beneath the smooth voice, within.*

What glorious possibilities.

Acknowledgements

I would like to thank the editors of the following publications where some of these have appeared in some fashion –*Wild Goose Poetry Review, New York Quarterly, Cincinnati Review, Gumball, Hiram Poetry Review, Barnwood, The Melic Review, Shade, Apis-UK, Greensboro Review, Florida Review, Negative Capability, Whetstone, Askew, Z Miscellaneous, Chattahoochee Review, Cape Rock, Passages North, International Poetry Review, Montana Review, Third Coast, can we have our ball back,* and *Grasslimb Journal*.

I would also like to thank the following friends and mentors who help with countless revisions of the poems within – Larry Levis, Greg Pape, William Olsen, David Dodd Lee, Walter Bargen, C.E. Chaffin

Foreword

David Dodd Lee

Jim Zola's *What Glorious Possibilities* strikes a tone that argues against the possibility for joy—a melancholy sublime, the dark shine set forth by the particulars of a given life—and yet finds much that makes a life substantively pleasurable. The fact that suffering seems to bring out the diehard romantic in this poet is part of what's so poignant about this book. Like Jon Anderson and Larry Levis before him, Zola's domestic landscapes and haunted meditations are both comic and surreal. And yet his overall project, his autobiographical, no-bullshit work, is a luminously beautiful acknowledgment of the human struggle toward the inevitable end of things. It's also, however, a testament that the lived life is more than just worthwhile—that we are blessed in being allowed to live at all. Zola's poems present a paradox. The idea that language can do nothing about this condition of our common humanity stands in stark contrast to the spark and soulfulness that burns on every page of *What Glorious Possibilities*. It has been almost twenty-five years since this poet has graced us with his vision (his only published book so far is 1990's *One Hundred Bones of Weather*). On the evidence presented here, I believe, and pray, we will be hearing from Jim Zola again, and soon.

For Trish

Contents

Acknowledgements
Foreword

1. The Human Arrow

Blues	15
Nobody Dies In This Poem	16
In the Night Still Dark	18
Darwin's Finches	19
Forecasting	20
How It Happens	22
Think of the Buzz, Think of the Sting	23
And it Stoned me to my Soul	24
My Mad Wife	25
You Ask Me to Write You a Love Poem	26
Voudoun Tale	27
The Long Winter	28
Unspoken	30
Revolt of the Landscape Crew	31
Confessions	33
Going	34
The Boy Who Wandered	35
The Disappearance	37
Summer	38

2. My First Book of Planets

Lost	41
Pied	42
Pig	43
Buddy Hackett in Heaven	44
Dolls	45
What Saint Francis Might Say To the Cockroach	
Under My Microwave	46
Quadragesima	47
Night Watchman	48

The Bee-Bearded Man's Only Son	49
After Watching Grackles Peck Green Apples Rotting on the Ground	50
In the 20th Town of Ghosts	51
What We Inherit	52
When Henry Grabbed the Live Wire	53
My First Book of Planets	54
Blue Barn	55
The Gangsters of Old Town	56
Frogs in Heaven	57
The Gardener Slips Out	58
The Gardener's Wife	59
The Ornithologist Leaves a Note	60
Who's On First or the Mystery of Harper Lee	61

3. Looking Up

After the Rain	65
Looking Up	67
Grasping Nothing	68
Instead of Attending a Reading by Billy Collins, I Go to the Zoo	69
The Author Visits Ms. Lafleur's Kindergarten Class	70
King of the Mountain	72
Under the Influence	73
With Buster Keaton and Hieronymus Bosch in my Head	74
Learning to Fall	75
Upside Down Love (after Sharon Olds)	76
The Roofer Stays Up	77
For Nothing	78
Last Words of the Man Who Read Dictionaries	79
Easing Into Dementia	81
Freebird	82
The Lessons	83

About the Author

1. The Human Arrow

Blues

It's not 1963. Still, heaven
is a Falcon, sky blue with rusted chrome.
It's not how, but where
and why. The town beach after a day
butterflying jumbos at the Fish Market.

A girl with tan shoulders, a fisherman's
daughter. Cheap beer, but what does it matter
after the first, the second. Who's counting?
Not the fisherman who dreams of Tautog
for chowder, walking the flats. His daughter

dreams of a wedding without sand. You ignore
dreams and drive to get gas, to watch a man,
maybe 5 years older than you, rub a rag
across your windshield as if the salt and grime
might actually disappear. His name

is on his shirt. Soon he disappears. But you
aren't interested in the schedules of grief.
Good grief the cartoon shouts. Yes, it's good.
She becomes your wife. In a few years,
her blood talks back to her, resists, the way

a three year old does after a day
at the beach, exhausted, refusing
to acknowledge sleep. Says *no*. Big Blues
eat the little Blues. Deep below,
something joyful swims out of it all.

Nobody Dies In This Poem

     The capital of begonia is pollen.
     The capital of whatever is why not.
     The capital of hunger is nuggets.

Jennifer comes to work flush-faced. It's 96 degrees and she has high blood pressure. After an hour, her skin is a cloud. I tell her *go home, relax, take your medicine.*

     The capital of tuxedo is holy.
     he capital of locust is vibration.
     The capital of wax paper is sweet.

I wonder if sending Jennifer homeearned me a few extra tokens towards heaven. Later, I smack my kid on the back of the head, not too hard, for doing something or not doing something. I figure I'm back to where I started.

     The capital of myopia is yellow.
     The capital of H-bomb is dandruff.
     The capital of magpie is silverweed.

I stopped taking my medicine years ago, for reasons that made sense then. Now my wife tells me I'm tempting fate. I carry a feather in my pocket. I swallow pins. My stomach rattles when I walk. The feather says nothing.

     The capital of Maine is Augusta.
     The capital of my name is J.
     The capital of this is this.

I have this sickness where I create people and give them lives. I care about them more than people I really know.

Mrs. K drove her Bug
into a streetlight. I write
her a sympathy card. Mr. N
has cancer of the fingernail.

I can't sleep at night. Nobody
dies. I repeat this until
the air around each word implodes.

In the Night Still Dark

The leaves have drawn out
their dying. Just as I

let myself linger.
I'm the grumpy General,

barking orders about gloves
and hats. Putting on

a sock, my son forgets
what world he's in. I can't

forget. I keep notes
in my pockets.

The snowy owl peers
down the sweetgum branch,

a license plate reads
soon. Later, after

the house settles
in its dark reluctance,

after the owl's belly
is full of mouse, leaves

start to crash against
roof and windows.

Darwin's Finches

My son sits in the rocking chair
writing thirty times *I will not do....*

On the couch my daughter reads to me
from a book about firefighters.

She uses this voice when reading aloud
like air that sets on the sill the first time

you open the window after a hard winter.
Outside you hear birds you can't see.

Maybe finches. Still further off,
a siren yawns. My daughter rises

like smoke. My son wears a look that says
I know I shouldn't, but must.

Forecasting

I wake to a wound I touch
and forget, to water pipes
that freeze and burst, to the cry
of a child who knows the world
is his for now. This could be

any town, with poolhall light
spilling yellow on ringers
propped against the church wall,
as if the odds were simple,
where redbuds burst in graveyards,

then along streets, warehouse birds
hop from corrugated rooftop
to dying elm, and towheads
wait for a train to bend a penny,
where no one hears the river

press smooth muscle against banks,
the bluffs tumbling to plundered tracks
where a breeze is a blessing.
We blame what we can
on the river and sleep

with coins on our hearts
to ward off dreams, this life.
At night, when you cry
and will not stop, I say
anything – this loaf of bread

is the face of god,
or promise to take you
to the fields beyond
the half-built houses,
where cowbirds sing.

If you stare long enough,
the cows sing too. I tell you
about rivers, how the Mohawk
is the birth of loneliness,
its locks bloated with dark water

and fish we could not catch. I lift you
to the window, to the lights
flooding Paris Road, the stars.
Some nights I let you cry
and hold my eyes shut as if

I could keep sleep in forever.
Other nights, you wake
and don't cry, and I hear you
singing a song that says
this is the weather I was born into.

How It Happens

One night the world seems right
moon in place
the dog snoring
lightly at the foot of our bed

By morning the faucet in the bathroom drips
it didn't before
I resort to my usual tools
my phillips screwdriver
my red plumber's wrench

my curses and pleas
This is the next to last straw

a broken lace on the shoe of madness
you laugh say
a cockroach can live for days

without its head
Then I'm tapping a tune on the pipes

La Cucaracha
and you are shimmying naked
down the hallway.

Think of the Buzz, Think of the Sting

My wife wants to make love in an ocean of bees.
Think of the buzz. I think of the sting. Out back,
my neighbor with his six year old son is digging
in the hard winter clay. They stand over the hole.

From here, they appear solemn, silent. But this
just might be a trick of distance and light. Maybe
they are sharing a knock knock joke, or reviewing
names for the next batch of fish even as Goldie floats

towards heaven. I love the way children are so quick
to name things, small gods that they are. I also love
how easily they forget, ten minutes from now
the son will be back playing dinosaurs

or intently sipping a juice box, without sorrow.
The father washes dirt from his hands and feels
an unnamed ache throughout the day. And I,
stranger, will keep this scene for a long time.

Until I make love in an ocean of bees,
after the buzzing that comes when all living is done.

And it Stoned me to my Soul

When you were born,
Airiana the Human Arrow
flashed across the Coliseum's
buttery air, hawkers sang
for money. You flew.

I'm tired of the bitter river.
My love is like a canker sore.
You'd hug your tormentor's waist,
my only daughter.

My Mad Wife

It took me years to realize her madness,
though she is sweet and good-hearted.

Though she lifts the snapped mousetrap
with a spatula. Though she forgives the dish,

the floor that broke it. I read water rings
on the coffee table, shredded scales of straw

wrappers from juice boxes, the misspoken
body alphabet, her lips pursed, her purse

on the bedroom floor leaking receipts.
With borders thinner than sanity,

she is able to hide her madness.
At first it made me angry, her twin.

Made me look left of her, at clocks, clouds,
places I couldn't see. I wondered

if others noticed. She wears it
like silver toe rings. Though she smiles, nods,

talks in duplicates. Yes, yes. Though she
touches the burnt bulb and believes in light.

Though she strings little bibles.
Though she doesn't love and loves too much.

You Ask Me to Write You a Love Poem

The overhead light flickers a tempest
in my kitchen where I sit at the old
wooden table and try to write

about you or the sky. Nothing comes.
I think about the horses
Spanish explorers brought to the new land,

strapped up and blind-folded for weeks on end.
Finally, reaching the far shore,
taken out of the ship's belly,

they were reborn. I imagine they could barely
stand and must have thought sunlight was fire
from heaven. Blinking

into the new light, wobbly-legged,
amazed to be alive.

Voudoun Tale

A man sits down to a table and explodes.
Bits of him float from the ceiling covering
his family like feathers, spicing their food.
In Haitian there are twenty-seven words
for fire and none for snow. The undead walk
through coals and don't leave footprints. They work
the cane harvest for no pay. It's difficult
to tell who is who in the fields.

I put sugar in my coffee and wait for my heart
to race, ready to confess all my sins
to no one. An empty house has no ears.
I write fire on paper twenty-seven times
and feel the heat. My scalp snows my shoulders

How many times have I attempted to leave?
I sit in my car, listen to Blues For Pablo
hissing somewhere almost beyond the radio's
reach. Once I got as far as New Orleans
where a loony nag on Magazine Street
told me my eyes were not right
then asked for a dollar. I had two.

Three times I think. The rest of the time,
I drift like feathers from the ceiling.
I love a woman I do not know. I write snow,
it turns to fire. I know a woman I do not love.
Footprints and shadows.

This is no tale familiar.
This is not the story of my life.
A poet sits at the table and explodes.
There is no family to notice.
Or not notice.
The room slowly fills with silence.

The Long Winter

During the fall of earthquakes and tropical storms,
when trucks rattled the windows and a breeze
through the floorboards told of winter,
when the thick fur on the dog's neck
made it certain, when the first frost left
the pepper plants wilted with half-ripe fruit
we set on a windowsill until they released
the sweet smell of too much waiting, when all
the signs were right, when birds tucked wings and slept
or learned to sing in the dark, as if the sun
could forget or half the world could forgo
sleep; then you were conceived, and the sun
cast its shadow across a single leaf.

Sometimes the signs are wrong, the days too warm
for jackets. Then my thoughts are with names
and naming, the way we are certain
it makes a difference, this Herbert, this Elisa,
as if a sound can change what we grow into.
No matter. You will forgive us
in a room we won't see, waking from a dream
as soft as the light in the tiny office
of the truck terminal across the street from me now,
where trucks run half the night
while drivers make calls and wait,
as I wait for the sound of wheels
rolling through gravel and white soot: I wait
to give you stories – a mother wearing the mask
half-way through September, father believing
in a cure, web across the wound, pine-top
needles, the color of your sprouting hair.

You won't believe me or the light shining yellow
across the street, the trucks loaded with peppers,
three days from ripe, ready to go.

Unspoken

You ask the sign for beauty.
Take your open hand, palm towards
your face, and circle once, ending
with the fingers together as if
drawing what's inside out.

Nowadays I lean in to catch
words, then nod and smile
even if I don't know
what was said. We laugh
and blame our decadent youth.

Alexander Graham Bell invented
a hearing aid for his deaf wife.
On his deathbed, she leaned in,
whispered *please don't leave me*.
He answered with the sign for no.

Revolt of the Landscape Crew

The council rules against noise,
looks towards us as they fine-tune
phrases; aware of the shadows
we cast on their manicured lawns.

They want to take away
our blowers. The bosses barely blink.
There are more able bodies
to fill the pick-up trucks.

These days the talk above the din
of mowers is less jingo,
more muted sputtering.
I invite the clouds, watch drops

wet asphalt, concrete. We sit
in the Texaco shop, sip
scalded coffee and flirt
with Alyce whose two-inch nails

provide a focal point
between the muffins and the swell
of her uniform.
We never talk of rebellion.

It's in the dark moon under
our fingernails, the whispers
outsiders don't trust, the way
we hold a hoe and barely bounce

in the back of the truck, stare
into mini-vans. It's strange --
there are no children
in the neighborhoods we work.

Just dogs we never see that bark.
And the parting of curtains.

Confessions

What gives with the wind today?
I feel its presence slip beneath
my collar, cuffs. Okay, yes,
I'm playing Emily again.
I haven't been out or felt

the angry wind. My face pressed
against panes of glass. In fact,
I haven't stepped beyond
the welcome mat for months.
It's my shoes, they've lost their grip

and lace. No, it's something more.
My wife brings me bags of wimpy
burgers and iceless sprite.
She brings stacks of newspapers
and magazines. I know the world,

each happening. Okay, so what?
I killed my wife, slipped inside
her sweet bay skin. Cursed, I have
no wife, no kin. I am the wind
creeping low around the arbor

and underneath a ladder
left by the hedge since fall. Scraps
pirouette, a soup label,
the neighbor kid's math,
some lover's X's and O's.

Going

I leave the going away party for Murray and drive
I-40 listening to oldies *–Why Do You Treat Me
Like a Worn-Out Shoe –* hypnotized by the patina
of rain. I'm at the train tracks used for transporting
lumber, walking my dog. Unleashed, I let her run.

She disappears for hours and returns covered in mud
and thistles, grinning as only a mutt can grin.
I stand in the living room. My mother is hanging
the only artwork of mine she ever so honored
in a wooden frame from Two Guys department store.
An ink fish I copied from National Geographic.

Fishing with my dad, a Flatbush boy unfamiliar with lures
and sinkers. He doesn't allow my sisters to go.
Just the boys. We sit on the cement walls of Lock Seven
dropping our lines into the dark water. I am two.
We have baby ducks that keep flying off the second floor

balcony, an Easter whim. We live upstairs.
Somebody lives downstairs but I never see them.
Later they disappear. The ducks. My father says
he let them go. Lost in the jungle of a yard.
Everywhere I turn is green, hedges that go

all the way up. Then I'm in this breathing machine.
Beneath my eyelids are paintings. Fish tickle my toes.
Each in and out is music. *Why Don't You Love Me
Like You Used To Do?* I hear a train whistle.
I'm not sure if it's coming or going.

The Boy Who Wandered

No matter the game,
we jawed the chance chill
from morning light like jays
who flit from power line
to elm's reach, all jingo
and practiced chatter.

When I was ten, a boy
dropped dead while playing
second base. They said
a clot stopped his heart.
He said he was tired
and lay down in
the middle of the game

in the middle of a day
so hot we saw heat rise
like a blanket from
the trampled dirt he chose
for a bed. Twenty years
later, it is as if
I wasn't there, as if

the story was told to me,
the way I tell my son
the story of the boy
who wandered too far, lost
in the woods. Eventually
they found him, alive,

in some farmer's field.
But he had changed, turned
animal, mute, unwilling
to stand. At night, when
the wind makes a language
of leaves and leans

against it; I become
that boy, the one who
wandered. The other boy,
the real one, I think of
less often. He was
a year older than I,

and so, still eleven
to those who remember
his face, his name. I don't.
Yet I remember
his voice rising from the day's
last dust, a playground

vesper. *No batter, no
batter, no batter. Swing.*

The Disappearance

One day you rise from a pile of newly raked leaves,
from the mouth of a dog, rise like a desire
to be pure, incurable, to forget
how we came to be here, to a world beyond
these neighborhoods where rushbeds slow the river,
where men who live nearby take razors
and soap to shave in front of marble churchwalls
twice destroyed by fire, where voices rise as one,
like smoke from a fire that will not flame. This could be
a street from an Ensor painting. Soon people
fill it, masked faces, skeletal, roundhousing the night,
as if they just discovered that none of their children
resemble them, or worse, that each child vowed to give back
their features, to resemble nothing.

Could the clamor of a single bell
drive the children deep through roots and creepers?
The bell is a story the townspeople tell
to explain the disappearance. As for the children,
they came out on the other side of the forest,
not to hallelujahs, but to second mortgages.
For them, the bell is the body ringing blood.
One day you rise from a flutter in the thicket,
from the cold hard dirt beside the resurging
Mohawk, from the cat's split open belly,
from the roe, rise and I don't recognize you,
though I hear the warning.

Summer

Mother makes me deadhead
portulacas all summer.
The rock garden is full of bees,
big drunk ones that won't take a hint.

My daughter holds her breath
past the graveyard, lifts her feet
across railroad tracks.
What August is this?

One where God is a hammer.
Where my daughter carries me
like a pail of strawberries
out of the dark forest.

2. My First Book of Planets

Lost

Because it's wet or green
or enraptured
the wood on the hearth
whistles.

Sister, your smile
is breadcrumb-laced.
Walls are pocked with gumdrops.
My stomach aches.

Whatever is in the oven
smells of burning hemlock.

Pied

The rat catcher drifts into town without a hat.
He winks, fiddles with his fife, sack slung across
a practiced droop, tells us about a tune,
a rodent rhapsody that fills the streets. He hones
his craft beneath a wilting willow, gnaws
the crust of week old bread until, exhausted
by the weight of his task, he snores, dreams
deep in tails and whiskers.

Boredom is our tableau.
We smash crab apples, dare bees to sting, bike
foreign neighborhoods hoping to lose our way.
One morning, we notice the brown patch below
the willow is shadowed by his absence. We guess
the rats left to cure their curiosity
by drowning. Come evening, some of us slow
our late-for-dinner gait just a bit,
cock an ear. One by one we disappear.

Pig

They said she would marry one from the North.
She did. But in bed, at night, she never felt
the hooves or kissed a snout. Still, each morning
he sat in feral pinkness, sipped his mug of mud.
Was it luck that brought the witch to her stoop,
that she took the hag's advice to thread a loop
around his ankle while he slept, to make him stay?
Instead, he left. The rotten cord broke. She realized
she loved the pig. Moon, Sun, Wind all sent her
packing. Three of this and three of that.
She wore out three pair of shoes and hauled
a sack of chicken bones. Finally finding
the place where her husband hid, she built a bone
ladder. While she climbed each fragile rung,
she must have cursed her sisters who married
Princes, her father who prodded her into this.
Dear Reader, I have no wish to resolve
this telling. Some say she cut her finger off
to finish the ladder top. What matters is
she married a pig. We all make choices.

Buddy Hackett in Heaven

Not allowed to stay up late
and watch, you listen
to monologues, gaffs, starlet
coos, punchlines below
the borschbelt.

Johnny won't tolerate blue.
The world spins on innuendo.

Now you explain to the kids how
there were only three choices,
a world made safe
by Deputy Dawg. Back then
you were in love
with the universe. Tell them
TV waves travel into space

and keep on going, and when
they ask for specifics,
change the subject. Buddy says
to Angel Gabriel,
a guy walks into a bar...

On some dead planet, Lucy
crams bonbons into her
everlasting mouth.

Dolls

On the radio, the Pope is explaining to the Indians of Haiti
how the magic of the old and the magic of the new do not mix.

He is talking about religion. You slam the door. We talk about
    love,
what is left of it at 4 a.m., hung over, not certain what we last said

or if the words belong to us. You once gave me wooden dolls
from Guatemala, told me about the magic passed from Mayan
    legend,

how each doll represents a trouble that will vanish if you sleep
with that doll under your pillow. I stored them in a painted box.

Years ago I lost the instructions. Now I'm not sure which doll
    cures
which trouble. This one could be for toothaches or world famine;

another, unwanted guests, phones ringing in the middle of the
    night,
departure. For days, I sleep with all the dolls under my pillow.

I only lose sleep. I try carrying them in my pockets when I go
to work. They are lost among the change. Late at night, I set the
    dolls

on the kitchen table and watch them. They do nothing. But I tell
    myself
this is to be expected and I take it as a sign. They don't seem
    worried.

I give them the names of every woman I've told I love. I whisper
    to each doll
you can tell me, I whisper *what's wrong, what in the world is the*
    matter?

What Saint Francis Might Say To the Cockroach Under My Microwave

Come out little life force, winged
crawler, currant on wheels. Come
share my toast with peanut butter.
I'll settle for the crumbs. Come out,
come out, from your safe haven.

I've forgotten the lowly sow,
her mooning, the calf's pathetic low.
It's you I want to lullaby,
your soul I long to marry
to the bottom of my shoe.

Quadragesima

like some monster loose in Your beautiful world
   – St. Augustine of Hippo

The martyrs meet in my dark kitchen.
fight for stools and coffee cups.
We niggle. Who cares if the Tyburn tree
is elm or maple? Let's concentrate
on transubstantiation, the origin
of infallibility. I put out blue
corn chips and salsa in the jar. The neon
light above the sink flickers and we stop.
Heresy the shorthaired mutt wants out.
No one moves. We bluster St. Francis
and his fever. No bliss on tap tonight.

I pray for wiggle room, an inch to worry,
and vow to give up abstinence,
the dark between my toes. What's left? Thirty-nine
more or less. The guys discuss real presence,
the grammar of St. Polycarp's last prayer
and if we need to meet again.
The tree was elm, the chips now crumbs.
The world waits for a reply. The dog barks.

Night Watchman

It's not the boredom that scares me, but these dreams
where I take off my uniform and discover
my skin is a uniform, my heart a badge.
This is my post – the night, apartments, cars.
A few trees define the landscape, their thin branches
point to what is not there. And I am thinking
of a woman who is like the trees,
but more distant – her name caged on the tip
of my tongue. I do not know her. She may live
in one of these apartments where light
and broken music taunt me. I want to think of her
all night, to learn how imperfect she is –
but two teenagers, a boy and a girl,
have hopped the fence to the pool and are swimming
naked, avoiding the glare of dusk-to-dawn lights.
I listen to whispers echo from the brick
of the buildings. I want to join them,
but this uniform hangs on my shoulders, my back,
grows heavier with each step I take towards the water.

The Bee-Bearded Man's Only Son

This is the day the bee-bearded man's only son is to wed
a girl from a town that knows nothing of bees.
The son himself feels no affection towards the bees,
but out of a sense of decency and heritage
has taken his father's trick one step further,
wearing a suit of bees and a top hat that sets the wedding crowd
to murmur. One fat aunt from Paducah faints,
and the men who know her gather round and bicker
about what should be done, until the question becomes moot
as she opens her eyes and mouths the word *yellow*.
The only clothing he wears not made of bees
are his Italian leather shoes because he's afraid
of what he might step on. The day is hot
and locusts hanging in trees make it difficult to hear
what the preacher is saying, something about hard work,
love and honey. No one listens. They are looking
at the bee suit, the way it moves constantly,
yet stays whole. The bride thinks about the coming night,
perfume between the breasts. She wonders if bees
get tangled in his hair. The son counts the moments
until he can shed his winged tuxedo. The bees
think nothing, drone, worker, all dying for the hive.
The father sips whiskey through a straw and considers
his toast – drinks held high to the first sting.

After Watching Grackles Peck Green Apples Rotting on the Ground

Sentimentality shifts like sunlight that hits
objects in a room throughout the day,

setting fire to a dinged lampshade, loved books,
the dog mid-twitch, dust defining the thinness

of air. When the devil comes, we'll fend him off
with a crabapple barrage like he has never seen.

In the 20th Town of Ghosts

What does it matter what reality is outside myself
– Baudelaire

Not even I am here.
The sun sweetens my pot of misery.

Every step I take leaves tiny graves.

The animals I recognize from dreams.

You stand in the back lit doorframe
pulling a silk robe across your chest, you explain

how the shed in the yard was built in anger.
I hear the argument of plank and nail.

As I open the one door, my life begins.

What We Inherit

When my father fell through the attic floor,
his legs dangling like a stuck bug, my mother
stood below and laughed. He patched the hole
the best he could. The crooked fix
is still there in the bedroom closet.
I visit, brood in tow, ten years older
than my father was when he stepped
where he shouldn't.

Never accused of being handy,
plumb lines distract me. I trust my eye
to a fault. Hung pictures tilt as though
I have one leg shorter than the other.
I give my sons the standard plastic tool kit,
pint-sized workbench better than my own.
They show an inclination towards
the hammered thumb, bent nail. I hope they find
a love who can laugh when they step beyond
the safety of beams to where the floor
no longer holds them.

When Henry Grabbed the Live Wire

The summer Henry died we went deaf
from the singing. At night when the cicadas
stopped, we stopped too, as if waiting
for a storm brewed from the quiet,
for the baritone of God to test us
with impossible tasks. Just as sudden,
the buzz restarted, a chainsaw needing
only one yank, orchestrated.

Walking the dog down by the railroad tracks,
each step exploded, wings crashing
into shins, thighs, or the unlucky
crushed beneath my heel. My dog spent hours
in pursuit, almighty hunter. Later,
he stood on stiff legs, stomach convulsing

one two three times and then out – a pile
of bile and bug. He sniffed and looked surprised.
As I imagine Henry looked when he clutched
the live wire, his body dancing.

My First Book of Planets

to truly understand
we must lie

a bruised moon
in the margins

surrounded by many
smaller objects

tiring of the dark
beauty

my wife's words flutter
from a cage

come to land on my head
surrounded by many

smaller objects
to truly understand

we must love the dream
we no longer carry

Blue Barn

Above the North Fork of the Black, the wind takes me
back to Blue Barn Road in Burnt Hills, New York –

a road named after a barn that burned to the ground
long before I was born, leaving only its name behind.

As a child I never thought about the building,
blue or otherwise, I roamed fields and vacant lots

where wind is the name of every ghost. Other children
were soldiers, letting their bodies dance into death.

I was an explorer. I read stories about John Ledyard—
how he feasted on whale, seahorse and bear

with the natives of Kamchatka; how he sailed with Cook
and drew pictures of Tasmanians – a people so simple

they had no need or name for fire; how he finally died
in Cairo, of fever, at the age of thirty-eight, calling for water

in a language the nurse couldn't understand. My Ledyard
days are over. Tonight, I stay out under the stars

long enough to gather the night's blue sigh. I build a fire
and think of all the sirens I have heard shriek by my rooms,

where the thought of disaster lasts only a few minutes
longer than the flashing lights. Out here, I watch the stars

and think of burning buildings. The cold gathers.
I feed the fire promises, a litany – *blue barn, blue barn.*

The Gangsters of Old Town

Wide-assed Buicks and dinged Cadillacs
navigate streets like big boats on a narrow sea.
We catch the occasional flash of a .45
over the dash before it transforms
into the shine of a freshly bobbed perm.

My mother brags she's not shrinking.
All of her friends look up to her.
The lady next-door asks to borrow
my books and I marvel at her quest
for knowledge until I learn how her thirst
is for light as she needs a step
to reach the switch.

But where are the old men?
Are they off losing coffee tin savings
playing pinochle with the dead?
Are they stuffed contently in rocking chairs
on so many porches, arms slightly raised
in a friendly eternal wave
to the old ladies driving by who might
smile back if they could see above
steering wheels as big as the moon?

Frogs in Heaven

Somewhere Bach is bashing out his brains
with a stolen 8th note.
American Encyclopedia of Decadence (revised)
has dropped me from its index.
Peepers know more than I know.

Keening virgins walk in line outside
my office of self-doubt. My files
are crammed with alphabetic flops.
Peepers know more than I.

I am stunned by an ankle in the aisle.
For want of a touch, the ankle
is turned between gentlemen darting.
Peepers know more.

So my spiritual energy is poisoned by seduction.
So I drag the flesh tattoo into an unlit street.
So I wash my face in the moon's gloom.
Isn't it best to ignore beatific visions?
Peepers know.

This is when the sky opens.
Golden anvils start to drop.

The Gardener Slips Out

My wife gathers roly-polies
from my pillow, leaves them in a dish
on the nightstand. She no longer questions
my humus cologne. I stem her prattle
with fresh cut aster, sprigs of salvia.
Some nights sleep avoids me. I become
a chameleon no one can see, slip outside
as if drawn by the flickering glow
of streetlight that has been there for years.
Or has always been there, just as the lank
weeds that edge the curbs have always been there.
Perennial. I stare into the yard

next-door, the spread of zoysia dew wet
and mowed too short, the unkempt beds.
I can't help it. I hop the fence to deadhead
mums and notice the yellow glow
at her window. How can she go so long
without thinning the clumps of hemerocallis?
Does she understand the dangers
of watering at night? I sense she watches
as I rest my head on her acrid soil,
testing it between my lips. I listen
for worm songs. My feet bleed; the blood
good for roses. By morning, they open.
She will dispute each bloom, snip them for vases.
By dark, I seal the stems with glue.

The Gardener's Wife

Just seven years old, I made a potion
in a terracotta pot. Blades of grass,
crabapple seed, dandelion puffs,
dried up peonies, other stuff.
The final touch -- three glops
of seasoned muck stirred
with a hickory stick and stuck
in a sunny spot to cure.

I made a vow. My husband doesn't know
I know. Today I found a spoon
half-buried beneath the dogwood tree.
He tries to hide his musky breath
with shots of whiskey. I see seeds
between his teeth, his boot prints deep
in other gardens. Some nights

before he leaves, still dumb with sleep,
I snake my hand beneath the sheets
and touch him and think this is the way
to make him stay. When we first married
his passion was like an anger on top
of me, a scowl, hands clenched beside
my face, dirt deep beneath each nail.

The woman next-door meets me at the fence.
Anchored by our coffee cups, we chat
about the latest blooms. She knows I know.
I have no use for pity. I think
about potions black as pitch and rich
as home-brewed coffee.

The Ornithologist Leaves a Note

When I realized I had lost my ability to think
in symbols, birds flew out of my head. Nothing fancy,
exotic. Common birds that children on playgrounds
name in rhymes. I keep a book on birds beside my bed,
a book on trees, on plants, stars as if I might forget
I live on this earth. When you remind me (there is always a you)
that blue flowers are a part of life, your words are like rain
crossing a lake. I want to dive under before the drops reach my
side

where I stand on the bank full of things I cannot see.
Once I could see more than this, the way light and shadows
are unashamed, the way I desire to live in-between life.
You say that observation is not enough. The fly trapped
inside the window frame now (there is always a now)
might agree. Suffice to say birds flew out of my head today.
The last one had no feathers and wore a jacket made of blue blue
flowers.

Who's On First or the Mystery of Harper Lee

Who savors the essence of infield grass,
relishes the breeze of the swung bat.

Shadows encroach the alley, crowds hush thin.
What sports a pissed mug, cheeks dribble brown.

The battery marks time with gentle lobs
and signs no longer secret. They meander.

Who observes how *I Don't Know*, guard
of the hot corner, gently pounds his glove

kept oiled all winter. The board blares
goose eggs, bleachers echo ennui,

a wave without beginning or end.
Tomorrow fingers the pill's seam, contemplates.

Who tips his cap to *Why* and *Because*
in left and center. Right remains a mystery.

Could be Miss Harper Lee for all we know,
peppering the opposition with innuendoes,

shyly graying under artificial light,
dedicating her next dinger to Mister Capote.

3. Looking Up

After the Rain

My father's funeral lasts forever.
First the wicker chairs on the lawn turn black,
legs crumble. Then the grass gives up. We stand
and rock from foot to foot, fold hands.
Look at the sky my mother says. I look
at her mouth. When the rain begins, we rush
for umbrellas, cars. Except my father.
He pouts. *Where's my body? Why are my shoes
filled with ash?* When it stops, I'm sixteen,

drunk, sneaking into the house. My shirt's stained
with Norman's garage brew. I've lost my shoes.
My mother and father are watching the news,
the weather. I stand there, try not to sway.
My feet grow roots. My father has no face

as he lifts me, carries me to the car.
We've spent the evening at the Aceto's.
The adults drink downstairs while I play upstairs
and listen to the music of their laughter
rise like smoke that puts me to sleep.
It's like a miracle the way I close
my eyes in one place and then wake
in another, at home in my own bed.
Maybe I stir just a little as my father
sets me in the car. But sleep is what I want.
It's not a dream my father tells me.

No, I tell myself that death is like
that car ride. But this is all too easy.
I'm afraid that nothing is how
I imagine it. Drunk on wine aged for days,
puke on the floor by my bed, my mother
hating my father for dying, my father
wishing he could open his mouth to let it fill
with rain. But he doesn't have a mouth.
And the rain hasn't started yet.

Looking Up

Father, who never hammered a nail straight in his life,
taught me how to curse the struck thumb. So I taught
my son. At the age of two in the tub he damned
his sinking ship.

Summers, as punishment for being a kid,
my father had me paint -- gray over peeling gray,
fences so rotten I could poke a finger through the wood,
and did. Bikes, chairs, window frames.

Slow strokes and frequent drip inspections. I left home
to work with a friend. House painters. We lied
about experience, gave ourselves a fancy name –
Carmichael Brothers, Painters Inc.,

although we were only Zola and Michaelson.
Our first job, I got stuck doing the eaves. I climbed
and realized my fear of heights. I clung.
Looking down I saw my father looking up.

Grasping Nothing

Because it's raining
I think of my grandmother's perfect blue perm,
how I wanted to touch it.
It would be easy to say
her hair was like the nests we collected
on the mantel. One had two halves
of a bright blue egg.

When it rained,
she covered her head with a scarf
or a plastic bag. My wife tells me
when she went to church as a child
all the girls were required to wear hats.
If they forgot,
mothers made them wear a tissue.

Last night I had a dream of undoing.
Someone tried to put the leaves back on the trees.
In the attic a toy piano plinks.
Then my grandmother comes down the stairs
as agile as a floating tissue.
She's laughing, telling me
to go ahead, touch it, boy. When I reach out,
I'm surrounded by the suddenness of wings.

Instead of Attending a Reading by Billy Collins, I Go to the Zoo

No bears are there, brown, grizzly or polar.
The lion looks right through us, a yawn.
Seals sleep at the bottom of the artificial
ocean. Gorillas loll on their backs, ripe
for tummy rubbings. I lose three straight
staring contests to my daughter over salty fries
at the Jungle Junction. The highlight
for my son is the warthog pooping
by a bush. *Wasn't that so cool? I could smell it.*
He'll remember this more clearly than my face.

Just the way I remember the folds of skin
on an ancient walrus at the Berlin Zoo.
Driving home, backseat snores make happy
harmonics. Later, you ask me to join you
in the shower. Though it isn't sex you want,
I picture giraffes attempting to hump.
I think Billy would agree that this is the image
to end on. So why do I insist on ending
with the rhino's dusty horn?

The Author Visits Ms. Lafleur's Kindergarten Class

A lick of air passes over me, the same
breeze that once touched Gauguin's

colorful knuckles as he tweaked the raisin
nut nipple of some young girl whose life

didn't warrant a footnote. The teacher
tells the class how they must write a story

with a beginning, middle and end.
They are in kindergarten and I am

their special guest. They struggle
to stay criss-cross applesauce,

while the bushel looms so wide
and curious. My stomach grumps

at the thought of a just picked Winesap,
juices on my chin, and I find myself

staring at the teacher whose denim jumper
holds some other fruit. I picture her

in my garden snipping the heavy blossoms
of a late blooming peony, to put

in a crystal vase her mother gave her,
and place upon the kitchen table.

When the lazy curse of morning lifts,
I lift her jumper. We test the strength

of the table. Afterwards, I brush the crushed
petals from her back. She says my name

and the roomful of children clap.

King of the Mountain

When I was ten and still unbeaten, I would cry out
to no one, or to myself –I am King of Everything –
and it was true. I claimed all I touched, and more;

even shadows bowed, though my own barely filled its dark shape.
King of the mountain, of grass waiting to sprout into certain fields,
of the day's last light taking all we knew with it,

of the way everything moves apart, together. Now,
there are times when I drive all day, past houses with windows lit
by what I imagine inside, past the shadows of strange-limbed trees

and shadows of the men who once cut a path through such trees.
I follow roads that end at bars. I forget the names. It's the shadows
that attract me – the way cool air allows itself to go into
    everything,

until all that matters is that once, in a bar in New Orleans,
I watched an ex-welterweight – a would-be contender
if not for the losses – take himself hostage in a corner,

a gun pointed at his shadow, at the shadow's heart,
shouting *It's mine,* until a friend talked him into surrender,
taking away first the weapon, then, for a while, the dark.

Under the Influence

A blowsy woman weaves parrots
and never smiles. Or if she smiles,
it is in the dark
of her lover's hair like whiskey
and trouble, like loosely braided
love. There are gaps in this logic,
peeled back to reveal the circuits
we learn to trust, the road that curves
until we know without looking
each downshift,
until we are under it all,
the bramble of gears and blossom,
the secret maps, under the ground,
the place where all we fear turns
into water and then back
to what we believe.

With Buster Keaton and Hieronymus Bosch in my Head

Sky drizzles cars
With headlights on
The street is a painting
Of a black and white movie

My lover calls on my cell
To tell me she's holding
Herself hostage
Tapping the butter knife on the counter
As proof

This morning I take my car into the body shop
A vicious mutt strains at a chain
The sign on the window says
Deliver all packages to the tattoo shop next-door
A man with a wrench the size of the moon
Smears grease on the one spot of his face
Still white
We'll take care of you he smiles

Meanwhile the streets threaten to mute
Back into cliché

I frown myself happy
Afraid to look up

Where a naked nun rides a fish across the horizon

Learning to Fall

I lean into the crisp white
uniform of the nurse.
Closer she says. Take off
your shoes. Sing like a cricket.
She pinches the fat of my back.
Stand on one foot. Tell me
what you were doing before
you fell. After. I fall
in love with her thick wrists.

For therapy, they make me fall
in odd situations.
Each time, I fall harder.
They take photographs. Later,
they accuse me of not trying.

They tie weights around my legs,
my arms, push me into cool water.
For a while I'm floating.

Upside Down Love (after Sharon Olds)

I stand on my head after making love
white flesh untesting gravity
hair up there now down unswept
sweeping the kitchen tile

arms trembling complaints --
we've reached the floor, what's next? --
my sex out of the scene
why in the kitchen where we seldom eat?

my feet on top like glorious beagles
ignoring the yips and yaps of socks
abandoned in another room
where is the artist to capture

this upside down love?
she's in the doorway laughing
laughing laughing holding her sides
waiting for the collapse

The Roofer Stays Up

I sit atop this roof after the last
shingler has tossed his last wisecrack
to no one. Across the street, a couple
hesitate in the doorway between
the hushed dark of the house, a brush
of streetlight. I suppose they are lovers
because I am alone. I suppose
that when they spill into the furnishings
of their lives, they'll touch at the wrist.
Just as I suppose this night will stay
like lovers who stifle their cries
with silk scarves because walls are thin,
windows left open. By morning,
when others arrive, I'll say
I came in early to avoid the heat.

For Nothing

No honest poet can ever feel quite sure of the permanent value of what he has written, he may have wasted his time and messed up his life for nothing.
   –Jean Cocteau

Somewhere behind the row houses, between the uncut
and dying grass, a dog twitches, dreams of deer,
an old man blinks into small fires, a woman carries groceries
like a grudge into a house wallpapered by the cry of birds.
I think about bodies, the way it took years to know my wife
this way, this map of turns and flesh. I know when she wears
silence like a coat that I must check each pocket. I know
I cannot teach or tell my kids the things they need to know. My son
talks about playing his game until he's dead, which means forever.
My daughter looks at me and asks why I look so sad. I don't tell
   her.

Yesterday the sun came back. Puddles in the yard turn into mirrors.
Bela the dog licks from a bucket filled to the brim.
So much depends on the weather. My scars ache, turn dark.
Two chickadees splash in a shallow bath. The world keeps
tumbling forward.

When I was a child my job was to burst the spent blooms
of portulacas clustered low along rock walls.
Timing had to be perfect, not too freshly gone
or the seed wouldn't drop and spread between cosmos
and dahlias. If I waited too long, bright yellow finch would feast.
I took my task seriously and kept an eye out for snakes,
red touching black, friend of Jack.

Today two crows flew into high elm branches and sat
fussing their cry for all within hearing, a broken song
of joy thirty feet up, to say – look,
even my gardener stops his weeding to listen.

Last Words of the Man Who Read Dictionaries

Eventually he had to let words go,
as if his left frontal cortex
were a bucket of golf balls. Every time
he added one, another popped out. At first
it was smaller words like *lep* and *vex*
and *pod*. He had to look-up *bosh*
two days consecutive – the lower
part of the sides forming an obtuse
angle at the bottom of a blast
furnace. He felt obtuse. It was gradual.
Second definitions slipped down
a papery slope. He no longer knew
that *blast* is a sheep disease
too in which the stomach and bowels
distend with air. Then one day the big boys
started jumping the gray matter ship.
Chiropterygium waved bye-bye,
hippiatry galloped free,
objuration vowed absence. The man
began to introduce himself as Mr. Tan.
It fell apart. Sky was bracky green.
Proper names scooted. His favorite teacher
from second grade, Mrs. Mars, turned to
what's-her-face. But he kept reading
dictionaries of music, tools, fashion,
abbreviations, mountain bike slang. His friends
stopped dropping by. One night his wife caught him
in the basement with a maglite
and a dictionary of sexual deviance.

He looked at her, his mouth shaped O,
oculolinctus he said. She blinked
and went to pack her bags. By morning
she and the dog, canis familiaris,
were gone. He lost all reason beyond
the alphabetic and took to bed.
When the doctor came there wasn't much to do.
The man's tongue was swollen. In the report,
the doctor wrote the man kept repeating
a bridge, a bridge. Then he crossed it.

Easing Into Dementia

Wait for the day you get lost on Main Street,
lost in your slacks and button down shirt.

You find yourself easing into your
father's slang, rubbernecking the icebox,

you bet your bottom dollar. Then your life
isn't worth a plugged nickel. You've earned

a ticket to Palookaville. All along the route,
you watch houses, beautiful houses,

disappear into the dark.

Freebird

I have this fantasy where I'm a poet,
white capped and famous. Using a poetry scale
of fame I'd fall somewhere below Robert Frost,
perhaps well known enough to be an answer
on a crossword puzzle. Fame wouldn't change me,
still out of touch with reality, still up
each morning to play with the dog, virtual fetch –
Good dog, imagine a stick. Fame hasn't brought me
wealth or comfort. Still, I no longer freckle with guilt
while reaching for the top shelf vodka at the ABC,
or practice my mantra – *sufficient, sufficient* –
while the clerk swipes my card. I am select
in accepting invitations to do readings.
Front rows fill with professors. It's the other rows
that gather my gaze; co-eds clutching my works.
I find myself no longer undressing them
with my eyes but instead adding lines to their faces,
a little gray and some weight. My new idea
of beauty. When I approach the podium,
I do so with a casual swagger, having left
the need for seriousness to the gents
in the front row. I smirk, clear my throat and ask –
are there any requests? – hoping, hoping someone
will be brave enough to shout out (a whisper won't do)
the clichéd response in a tone that rings of cell phones
held high flickering screen saver lighters in the dark.
Then I fumble through my loose stack of papers
although the one I want is always on top,
and after an appropriate silence, read this poem.

The Lessons

this is the place they take you in
wash your feet

you sip the water of forgetfulness
language is a spoon

a young girl squats to pee
behind the slaughterhouse

touches
the place the body forgets

they take you in
to send you out again

About the Author

Jim Zola's poems have appeared in journals and anthologies for many years now. He has served as poetry editor for The Melic Review. His chapbook, The One Hundred Bones of Weather was published by Blue Pitcher Press. He works as a children's librarian at a public library in North Carolina and for years also worked as a toy designer for a large toy company. He is married with three children and two dogs.

www.ingramcontent.com/pod-product-compliance
Lightning Source LLC
Chambersburg PA
CBHW070058100426
42743CB00012B/2587